Animal World

Animal Pairs

Patricia Whitehouse

Raintree

www.raintreepublishers.co.uk
Visit our website to find out more information about **Raintree** books.

To order:
☎ Phone 44 (0) 1865 888112
▤ Send a fax to 44 (0) 1865 314091
💻 Visit the Raintree Bookshop at **raintreepublishers.co.uk** to browse our catalogue and order online.

First published in Great Britain by Raintree, Halley Court, Jordan Hill, Oxford OX2 8EJ, part of Harcourt Education.
Raintree is a registered trademark of Harcourt Education Ltd.

Editorial: Nick Hunter and Diyan Leake
Design: Sue Emerson (HL-US) and Michelle Lisseter
Picture Research: Amor Montes de Oca (HL-US) and Maria Joannou
Production: Lorraine Hicks

Originated by Dot Gradations
Printed and bound in China by South China Printing Company

ISBN 1 844 21536 9
07 06 05 04 03
10 9 8 7 6 5 4 3 2 1

British Library Cataloguing in Publication Data
Whitehouse, Patricia
Animal Pairs
516.2
A full catalogue record for this book is available from the British Library.

Acknowledgements
The publishers would like to thank the following for permission to reproduce photographs: Barrett & MacKay Photo p. **12**; Byron Jorjorian pp. **5** (antlers), **13** (antlers), **23** (antlers); Corbis p. **21** (William Dow); Dwight Kuhn pp. **5** (tiger), **6**, **17**; FLPA pp. **19** (Minden Pictures), **21** (Jurgen & Christine Sohns); Michael P. Turco p. **9**, back cover (camel); Minden Pictures pp. **5** (penguin, Frans Lanting), **8** (Jim Brandenburg), **10** (Frans Lanting), **14** (Gerry Ellis), **15** (Frans Lanting), **22** (Tui De Roy), **23** (flippers, Tui De Roy), **23** (horns, Frans Lanting), **24** (Tui De Roy); imagequest3d.com (Carlos Villoch) p. **18**; Stock Photography p. **10**; Tom Stack & Associates p. **7** (Tom Stack), **16** (Joe McDonald), **23** (flippers, Joe McDonald), back cover (snake, Tom Stack); Visuals Unlimited p. **4** (Jack Ballard); Wanderlust Images p. **20** (Howie Garber)

Cover photograph of a white-tailed deer, reproduced with permission of FLPA (Minden Pictures)

Every effort has been made to contact copyright holders of any material reproduced in this book. Any omissions will be rectified in subsequent printings if notice is given to the publishers.

Some words are shown in bold, **like this.** You can find them in the glossary on page 23.

Contents

What is a pair?

Two things that match make a pair.

You have a pair of eyes, a pair of ears, a pair of hands and a pair of feet.

Animals have pairs of eyes and pairs of feet.

What other animal parts come in twos?

How many eyes do these animals have?

A tiger has a pair of eyes.

They are yellow and black.

A snake has a pair of eyes.

This snake's eyes are yellow and black, too.

How many ears do these animals have?

An elephant has a pair of ears.

They are big and floppy.

A camel has a pair of ears.

They are short and furry.

How many horns do these animals have?

A bighorn sheep has a pair of **horns**.

They are big and curly.

A giraffe has a pair of horns.

They are short and bumpy.

How many antlers do these animals have?

A moose has a pair of **antlers**.

They are wide and flat.

A reindeer has a pair of antlers.

They are long and pointed.

How many legs do these birds have?

A flamingo has a pair of legs.

They are long and thin.

A penguin has a pair of legs.

They are short and fat.

How many wings do these animals have?

A bat has a pair of wings.

They are covered with thin skin.

A swan has a pair of wings.

They are covered with feathers.

How many flippers do these animals have?

A sea turtle has two pairs of **flippers**.

There is a front pair and a back pair.

A seal has two pairs of flippers.

Animals use their flippers when they swim.

How many paws do these animals have?

A polar bear has two pairs of paws.

There is a front pair and a back pair.

A tiger has two pairs of paws.

Two pairs make four paws altogether.

Quiz

Which pair of legs belongs to the flamingo?

Look for the answer on page 24.

Glossary

antlers

animal horns that branch out like a tree

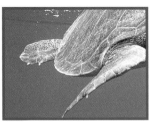

flippers

large flat feet that some animals have to help them swim

horns

hard pointed parts that some animals have on their head

Index

Answer to quiz
on page 22

Titles in the Animal World series include:

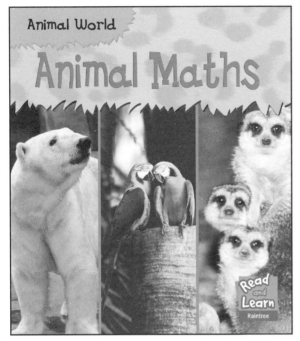

Hardback   1 844 21535 0

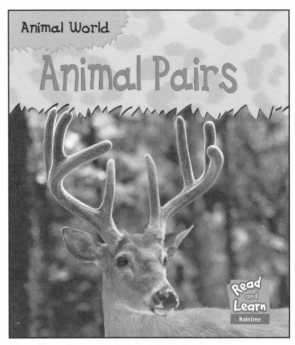

Hardback   1 844 21536 9

Hardback   1 844 21537 7

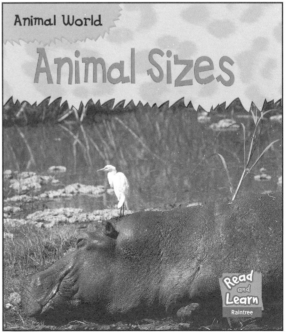

Hardback   1 844 21538 5

Find out about the other titles in this series on our website www.heinemann.co.uk/library